The Bucks

THOMAS NELSON PUBLISHERS
Nashville

A note to parents, grandparents, aunts, and uncles . . .

Millions of children celebrate Halloween each year with costumes, parties, and hi-jinks. But what are they celebrating? Where did these customs arise?

Some Christians strongly denounce any involvement in this spectacle of ghosts, witches, and evil spirits. Others wonder, "If it's 'All Hallow's Eve,' what in the world is 'holy' about it?"

The truth is that Halloween's deepest roots are decidedly pagan, and unlike Christmas and Easter, it has kept those pagan roots, despite its now Christian name. The controversy surrounding this holiday goes back well over a thousand years to when Christians confronted pagan rites of appeasing the lord of death and evil spirits. But the early Christians didn't simply speak out; they tried to institute a Christian alternative. All Hallow's Day (November 1) was a celebration of all "the holies"—those people who had died faithful to Christ.

Light against darkness. Life against death.

But Halloween in our culture has become an odd mixture of tributes to Draculas and roaming spirits, TV superheroes and comic characters, and participation in innocent harvest festivals and costume parties. Through the centuries, Christians of most persuasions have tried to transform this pagan holiday into a Christian one. How does one take a genuinely Christian stance today?

"Trick or treating" becomes a special problem. Children love the adventure of going out in costumes, but some parents have rejected trick or treating entirely. They argue that no matter how universal and supposedly harmless, "blackmailing neighbors for candy" is hardly appropriate. Instead, some create a wide variety of wholesome parties. Others carefully supervise their children as they canvass the neighborhood, perhaps having them add "God bless you" to their thanks for treats.

Certainly of all people, Christians should be joyful. The challenge is to use the creativity of the Creator to celebrate both the light and life He brought into this world, and His victory over evil—and evil spirits—which extends into the next.

To Brooke and Blake who bring joy to parenting.

Published in Nashville, Tennessee, by Thomas Nelson, Inc., Publishers and distributed in Canada by Lawson Falle, Ltd., Cambridge, Ontario.

Printed in the United States of America.

Library of Congress Cataloging in Publication Data

Myra, Harold Lawrence, 1939-
Halloween, is it for real?

Summary: A family discusses the origin of Halloween and its connections to paganism and Christianity.

1. Halloween—Juvenile literature. [1. Halloween] I. Walles, Dwight, ill. II. Title.
GT4965.M95 394.2'683 82-6323
ISBN 0-8407-5268-7 AACR2

4 5 6 7 8 9 10 - 97 96 95 94 93 92 91 90 89

"Eeyow! Ghosts!"
"Monsters! Spirits!"
"We're falling into graves!"
"Look out!"
"Ghosts are in the car with us! Grab 'em!"

"Hey, that was fun!" Todd exclaimed as they left the amusement park's haunted house. "What a ride! Let's go again!"

But Greg was very quiet. "I want to go back to Tom Sawyer's Island."

"Did the haunted house scare you?" Dad asked.

"Yes!" Greg answered loudly, "and I'm not going back. Not ever!"

"Aw, it wasn't scary, it was funny!" Todd insisted.

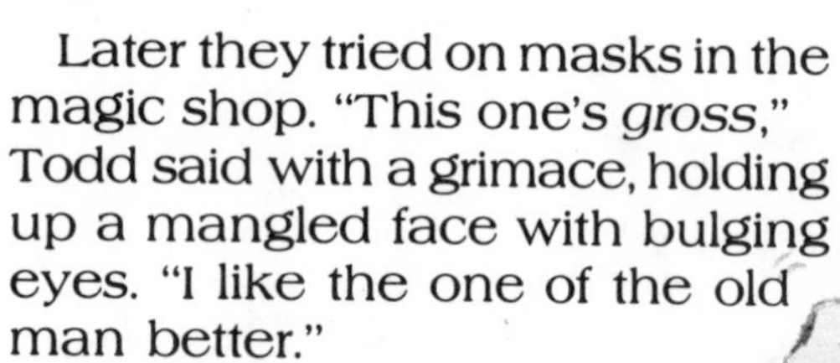

Later they tried on masks in the magic shop. "This one's *gross*," Todd said with a grimace, holding up a mangled face with bulging eyes. "I like the one of the old man better."

"For sure!" Michelle agreed. "Who needs this creepy stuff anyway? Greg's right about that haunted house!"

"Yeah," Greg said, sneaking a fake tarantula onto Mother's arm.

Michelle frowned at him. "Why do people love this stuff?"

"Because it's neat-o!" Todd answered.

Todd put on the old-man mask. "Next month's Halloween. I'm going to make a monster room with bloody bones and peeled grapes for eyeballs."

"Yuck!" Michelle said. "What's Halloween all about, anyway? All those horrible severed heads and dead people and ghosts! I've heard people say it's about the devil, and that we're stupid to celebrate it."

"Well, it *is* known as the devil's holiday," Mother said.

"How'd it start?" Todd asked. "Where'd all the witches and goblins come from?"

"It all started long ago—even back before Christ was born," Dad explained. "In what is now Britain and France, people called the Celts observed the end of summer with pagan rites. They believed a lord of death sent evil spirits into animals, who then roamed around all winter playing terrible tricks on people. To escape, you had to wear a disguise so that the evil spirits would think you were one of them."

"Weird," Michelle said. "Is *that* how the idea of wearing scary costumes got started?"

"Sure. And the pranks kids play now copy those of the ancient evil spirits. The Celtic priests—called Druids—offered sacrifices to the gods, and the people built huge bonfires on the hilltops."

"Sounds like fun," Greg said.

"Actually, more fear than fun! They lighted bonfires to frighten the spirits away. They even killed people in their rituals. It wasn't just toasting marshmallows and shouting 'Boo!'"

"Is that what Halloween means, then? Horrible evening, or something?" Michelle asked.

"Just the opposite," Dad said. "Centuries later, Christians came along and tried to change the holiday from a festival of fear to one of joy. October 31 eventually became All Hallow's Eve."

"What's that mean?" Todd asked

"It's a beautiful idea! 'All Hallows' means 'all holies,' or 'all the saints'—"

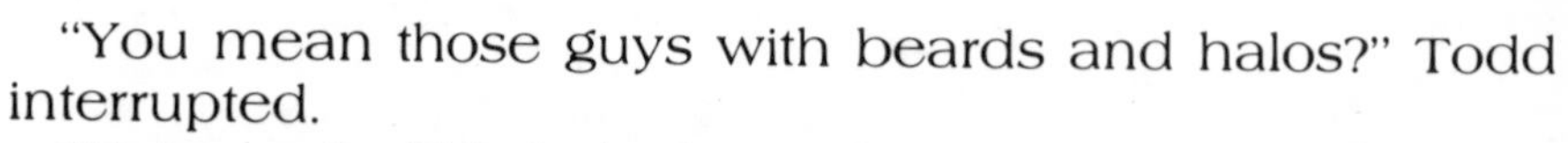

"You mean those guys with beards and halos?" Todd interrupted.

"Not exactly. This is the beautiful part. The Bible says every true Christian is a saint. We celebrate *all* saints. That means if you had a brother or sister or grandparent who loved God and died, you'd remember that person. You'd celebrate the joy those loved ones are experiencing in heaven and remember the good times you had with them when they were alive."

"Hey, neat!" Michelle exclaimed

"Do you think," Mother asked, "that Cousin Lois is happy in heaven? She loved Jesus very much."

"She still does!" Michelle said. "I'll bet she's having a wonderful time!"

"I thought Halloween was all about ghosts," Greg objected.

"In a way, you're right, Greg," Dad explained. "The Celts believed the dead would harm them. But we know that Christians who die are happy with Jesus Christ. Our loved ones aren't nasty ghosts. Don't forget—when Jesus rose from the dead, He had a *real* body. He walked, talked, touched things, and even ate fish!"

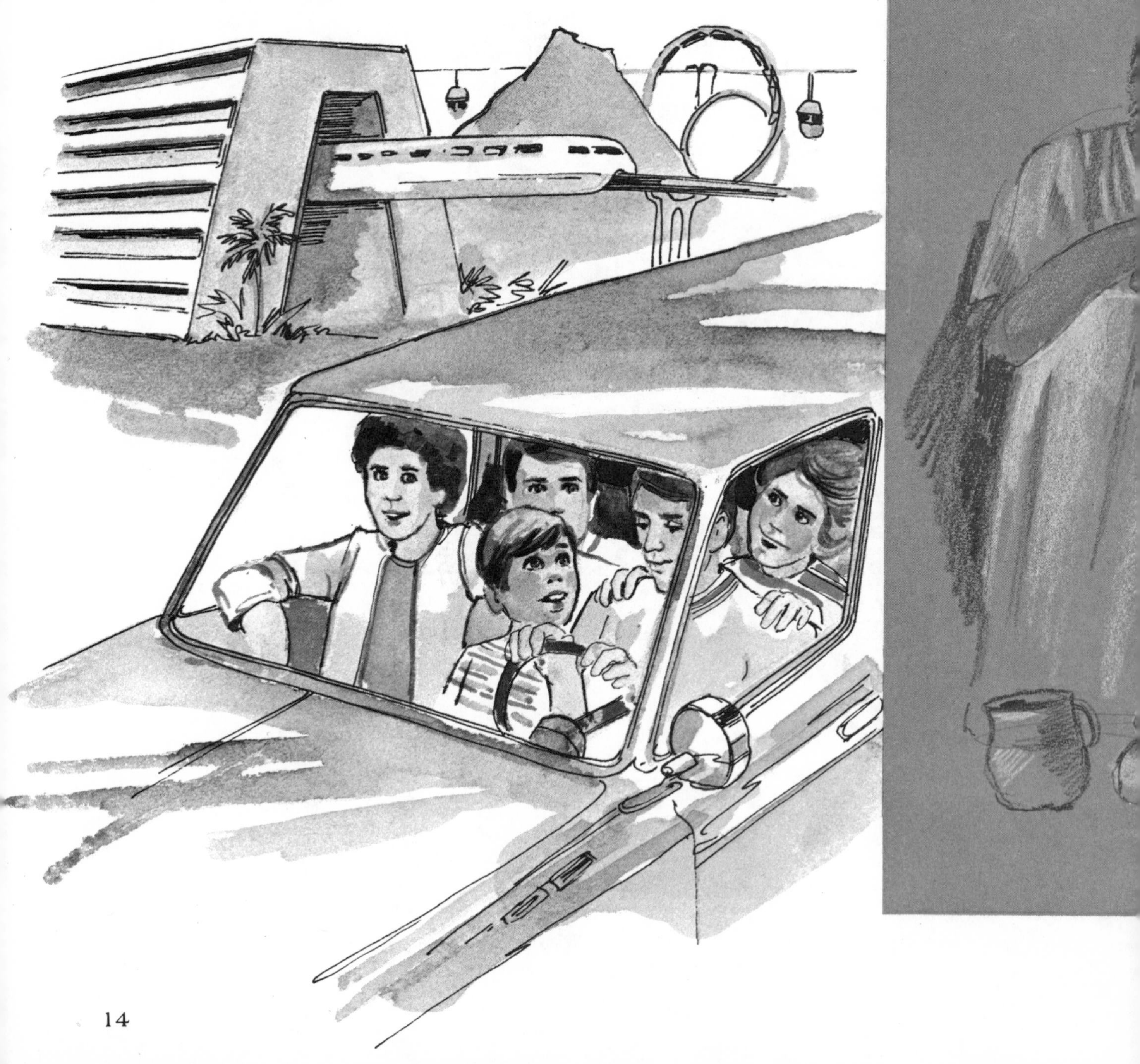

"If Christians changed Halloween so long ago, how come it's still about witches and skeletons and black cats?" Todd asked.

"Oh, the pagans just laughed at the church celebrations," Dad answered. "They made All Hallow's Eve into 'The Witches' Sabbath,' and they met to worship the devil. People were still frightened. Some waved pitchforks of burning straw into the air to scare witches away."

"That's silly," Greg said with a laugh.

"Sure is," Dad agreed. "Of course, today most people see this sort of thing as innocent fun. Witches, vampires, dungeons, and chains become nothing more than paper cutouts. Most people see soaping windows and overturning garbage cans as harmless pranks. They forget where all that came from."

"Well, what I'd like to know is how we can celebrate Halloween and not feel guilty," Michelle said.

"Let's have a festival this year at our house," Mother suggested.

"You mean with pumpkins and bales of hay and costumes and all?" Greg asked.

"Sure. And Dad can tell about Halloween."

Todd looked up at Dad. "You mean dressing like Dracula or a witch is okay?"

"Certainly not!" Michelle declared.

"Well, there's nothing wrong with my Captain Lightning suit," Greg insisted. "The Captain's a good guy!"

Michelle, Todd, and Greg were each allowed to invite four friends. So, on October 31, a lot of elves, hobbits, Indians princesses—and a Captain Lightning—were playing among the pumpkins and corn shocks in the backyard. What a sight!

They joined in all sorts of games and fun, including the silliest pumpkin-decorating contest the kids had ever seen.

Later, everyone jammed into the family room for cider, candied apples, and popcorn.

"Dad," Michelle said, "tell everyone about how Halloween started. I'll bet they've never heard about it before."

Dad told about the Celts and Druids, and how the early Christians celebrated All Hallow's Eve. "It's our time to remember the 'saints' we've loved. Actually, they aren't dead at all!"

A boy next to the fireplace said soberly, with a sad smile, "Guess that means Stacy."

All the kids had known his sister Stacy, who had died of leukemia. Dad smiled back at him. "Alan, it sure does mean Stacy. She loved Jesus very much. And remember the giraffe and elephant pictures she drew? And how well she could kick a soccer ball?"

"I even sort of miss the way she bossed me around sometimes," Alan said. "I really wish she were still here." He sniffed a little.

"It's natural to feel sad about loved ones who have died," Dad said. "Death is an enemy, and we miss our friends. But the Bible talks of streets of gold and the tree of life. The greatest adventure you'll ever have is going into the next world. Christians like Stacy who have gone there already link us to it even more."

"My grandpa died last year," Jamie said. "He taught me a lot about Jesus."

"Tell us about him," Dad said.

Jamie described his grandpa—how he had let him ride in his hardware delivery truck and how he had played the harmonica. Alan talked some more about Stacy and her stuffed animals and her butterfly collection.

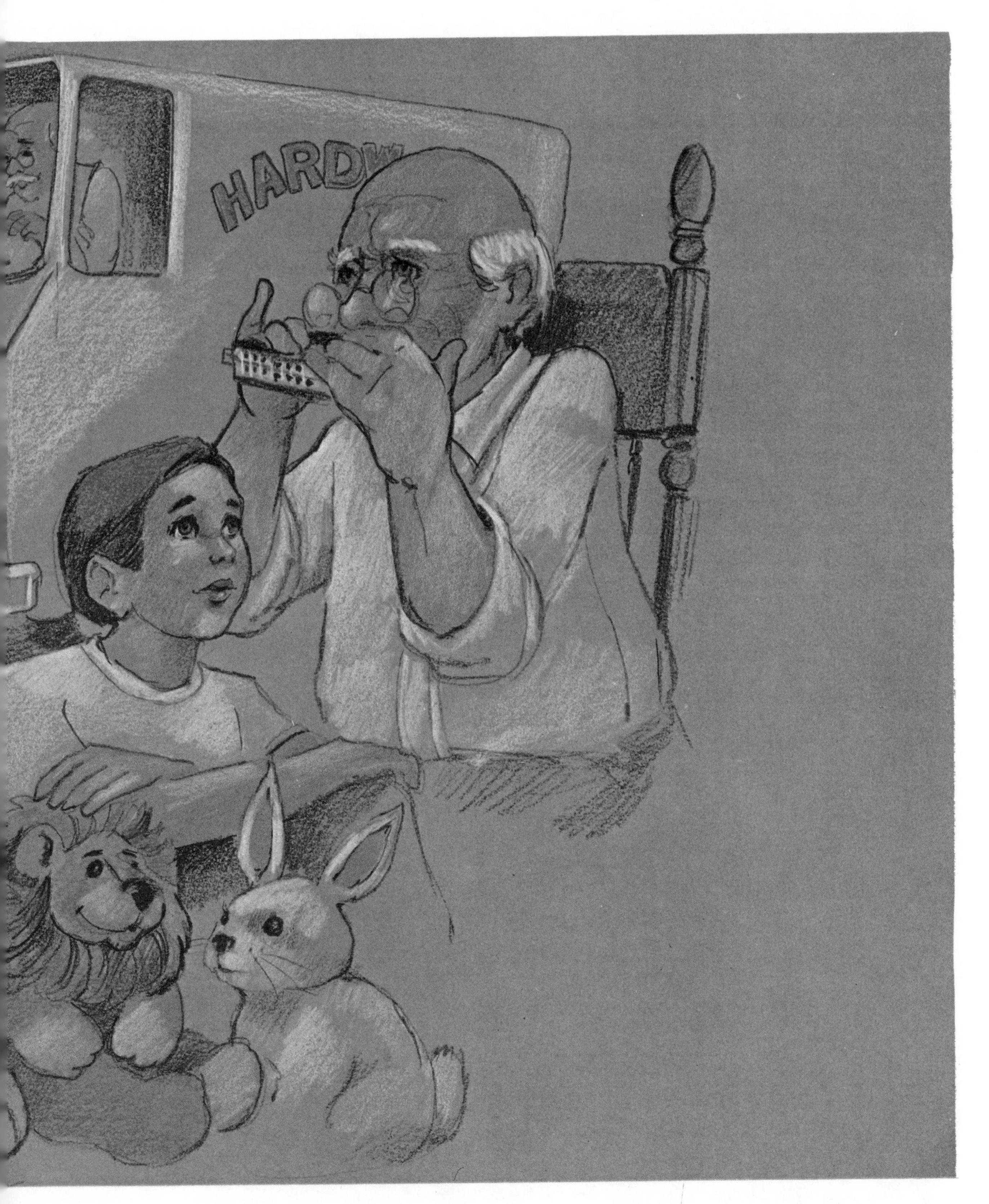

"We miss them," Dad said, "and it's good to remember them. But *they're* not sad; they're alive with Christ, awake in a different world."

A serious voice from a back corner said, "Maybe next year one of us will be there."

"We're all close to the next world," Dad agreed. "That's one reason it's so important to let Jesus take charge of our lives now. Christ has conquered the forces of death and evil."

Before leaving, everyone joined in singing songs about light and hope, finishing with "Amazing Grace":

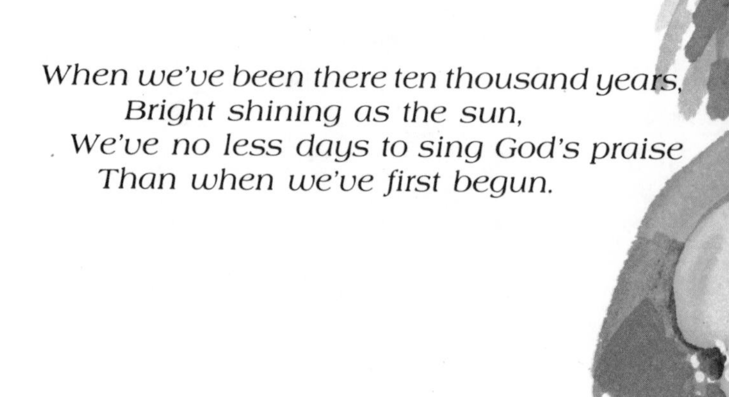

When we've been there ten thousand years,
Bright shining as the sun,
We've no less days to sing God's praise
Than when we've first begun.

That night, in his pj's, Greg said, "I'm still scared of ghosts! When I'm trying to get to sleep, the plant in my room looks like a monster, and I get bad dreams."

Michelle said, "Greg, when I pray about it before I go to sleep, I don't get nightmares." Then she asked, "But, Dad, how come we still like scary graveyard stories and horror movies, no matter how much we believe in Christ?"

Dad sat down and put his arms around the kids. "There *is* a supernatural world. We're fascinated by it, and there's nothing like a graveyard story to scare us awake! But evil does exit. That's why stories like *The Wizard of Oz* and *The Chronicles of Narnia* ring true. Temptations. Evil spirits. A lot of horrible things happen in this world. Evil powers are nothing to fool around with! But the Bible teaches us that 'God has not given us a spirit of fear, but of power and of love. . . .'"*

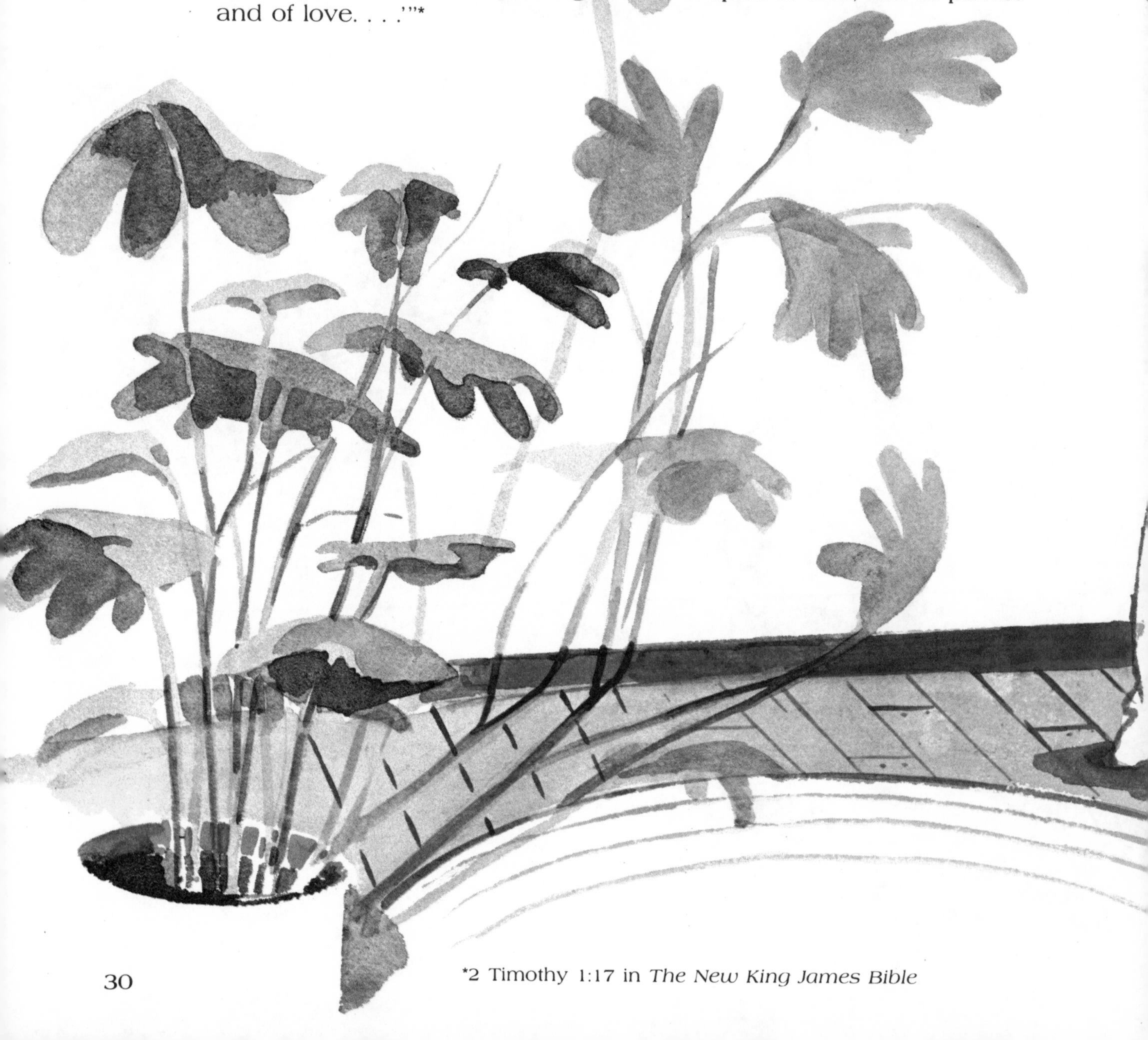

*2 Timothy 1:17 in *The New King James Bible*

That night, when gusty winds rattled the windows and the noises outside sounded scary, Michelle, Todd, and Greg snuggled under their warm blankets and smiled. They found themselves talking to Jesus about their thoughts and wondering if next Halloween could possibly turn out as well as this one had!